Endorsemen

"Christians are pressed by very real questions. How does Scripture structure a church, order worship, organize ministry, and define biblical leadership? Those are just examples of the questions that are answered clearly, carefully, and winsomely in this new series from 9Marks. I am so thankful for this ministry and for its incredibly healthy and hopeful influence in so many faithful churches. I eagerly commend this series."

R. Albert Mohler Jr., President, The Southern Baptist Theological Seminary

"Sincere questions deserve thoughtful answers. If you're not sure where to start in answering these questions, let this series serve as a diving board into the pool. These minibooks are winsomely to-the-point and great to read together with one friend or one hundred friends."

Gloria Furman, author, *Missional Motherhood* and *The Pastor's Wife*

"As a pastor, I get asked lots of questions. I'm approached by unbelievers seeking to understand the gospel, new believers unsure about next steps, and maturing believers wanting help answering questions from their Christian family, friends, neighbors, or coworkers. It's in these moments that I wish I had a book to give them that was brief, answered their questions, and pointed them in the right direction for further study. Church Questions is a series that provides just that. Each booklet tackles one question in a biblical, brief, and practical manner. The series may be called Church Questions, but it could be called 'Church Answers.' I intend to pick these up by the dozens and give them away regularly. You should too."

Juan R. Sanchez, Senior Pastor, High Pointe Baptist Church, Austin, Texas

"Where can we Christians find reliable answers to our common questions about life together at church—without having to plow through long, expensive books? The Church Questions booklets meet our need with answers that are biblical, thoughtful, and practical. For pastors, this series will prove a trustworthy resource for guiding church members toward deeper wisdom and stronger unity."

Ray Ortlund, President, Renewal Ministries

How Can I
Get More Out of
My Bible Reading?

Church Questions

How Can I
Get More Out of
My Bible Reading?

Jeremy Kimble

CROSSWAY®

WHEATON, ILLINOIS

How Can I Get More Out of My Bible Reading?

Published by Crossway
    1300 Crescent Street
    Wheaton, Illinois 60187

Cover design: Jordan Singer

First printing 2021

Printed in the United States of America

Trade paperback ISBN: 978-1-4335-7235-7
ePub ISBN: 978-1-4335-7238-8
PDF ISBN: 978-1-4335-7236-4
Mobipocket ISBN: 978-1-4335-7237-1

Library of Congress Cataloging-in-Publication Data

Names: Kimble, Jeremy M., 1980- author.
Title: How can I get more out of my Bible reading? / Jeremy Kimble.
Description: Wheaton, IL : Crossway, 2021. | Series: Church questions | Includes bibliographical references and index.
Identifiers: LCCN 2020041350 (print) | LCCN 2020041351 (ebook) | ISBN 9781433572357 (trade paperback) | ISBN 9781433572364 (pdf) | ISBN 9781433572371 (mobipocket) | ISBN 9781433572388 (epub)
Subjects: LCSH: Bible—Reading.
Classification: LCC BS617 .K56 2021 (print) | LCC BS617 (ebook) | DDC 220.6/1—dc23
LC record available at https://lccn.loc.gov/2020041350
LC ebook record available at https://lccn.loc.gov/2020041351

Crossway is a publishing ministry of Good News Publishers.

BP		30	29	28	27	26	25	24	23	22	21
15	14	13	12	11	10	9	8	7	6	5	4	3	2	1

Blessed is the man
who walks not in the counsel of the wicked,
nor stands in the way of sinners,
nor sits in the seat of scoffers;
but his delight is in the law of the Lord,
and on his law he meditates day and night.

Psalm 1:1–2

As a college professor at a Christian university, I want my students grow in their faith. I want them to see that theology is rooted in the Bible. I want them to see that the Bible is their greatest source of life and guidance. Ultimately, I want my students to love and understand the Bible.

But this can be hard. In one class, I illustrate the challenge by telling a fictional story about students who become passionate about God's word. Their newfound zeal prompts them to set out on the journey of reading the whole Bible in a year.

As they begin, they fly through Genesis. Who wouldn't? The story is compelling, the characters are intriguing, and many chapters play out like an ancient soap opera.

They move on to Exodus and . . . well . . . at least half of it is engaging!

And then there's Leviticus—the wasteland of broken resolutions and stalled-out Bible reading plans. About the time these once-zealous students reach Leviticus 5, their interest in the Bible has waned and their personal devotions begin to fade.

When I tell this story, students identify with it. Laughter, smiles, and a few looks of embarrassment fill the classroom. They too have been conquered by Leviticus; they've seen their good intentions to read Scripture fade away.

So what do we do about this? If you're reading this book, I assume you want to read the Bible more consistently. Even more, you want to *profit* from Scripture; you want God to increase your knowledge of him by his word. I want the same for my students, and I want the same for you.

Perhaps you've never meaningfully engaged with Scripture. Perhaps you relate to the story above and can't seem to get out of a Bible-reading rut: you resolve to read Scripture, stay consistent for awhile, miss a few days, fall behind on your plan, and eventually lay it aside altogether. Or perhaps you simply lack motivation to read the Bible because it feels a bit overwhelming or confusing.

My goal in this book is simple: I want to answer the question, "How can I get more out of my Bible reading?" I'm writing to Christians who want to know, love, and serve God. I'm writing to those who want to see the truth about who he is in Scripture. I'm writing for those who want to read Scripture better—or even those who just *want to want* to read Scripture.

We'll consider how to read Scripture in two sections. First, we'll focus on the surprising gift of the local church and how it teaches us to read our Bibles in more ways than we realize. Second, I'll provide some tips on personal Bible reading.

Why Read the Bible?

Before we discuss *how* to read the Bible more effectively, we should at least briefly consider why we should read the Bible. Consider the following truths.

- God exists (Ps. 14:1–2).
- God is perfect, majestic, and awesome in all of his ways (Deut. 32:4; Ps. 66:3).
- God created and sustains all things (Gen. 1:1–2:3; Isa. 45:5–7; Col. 1:15–17).
- God made us in his image to know him, represent him, and live for his glory in all our ways (Gen. 1:26–28; Isa. 43:6–7).
- God has revealed himself to us in Scripture (2 Tim. 3:16–17).

To summarize: the all-glorious God exists; made all things, including us, for his glory; and has revealed himself to us in Scripture. In 2 Timothy 3:16, Paul describes Scripture as "God-breathed" (NIV), that is, coming from the very mouth of God himself. Scripture is God speaking. As God's image bearers, our greatest need is to hear from him and align our lives with his purposes. We were made for this. We *need* the Bible.

Even more, the Bible tells us about Jesus and the promise of forgiveness that's found only in him. Without Scripture, we wouldn't know the good news of salvation through Christ.

You can see why Scripture is so important. The Bible is essential. It enables us to know, relate to, hear from, and acquire guidance from the God of the universe. We don't read Scripture so as to memorize and repeat religious mantras that will have some kind of magical effect. We read Scripture so God will transform our lives. We read so that we'll trust our Savior more fully, preserve unity among God's people, and guard sound doctrine. We read so that we'll know how to love and serve our brothers and sisters. We read so that we can love God and be transformed more and more into the image of his Son (Rom. 8:28–29; 2 Cor. 3:18).

Christians shouldn't read the Bible merely as a religious duty. We should delight in it, says the psalmist (Ps. 1:1–3). If my son only played soccer out of a sense of duty, his commitment wouldn't last very long. But he's been playing for years. Why? Because he loves it (though the snacks he gets after the games aren't bad either). Similarly, we read the Bible to know the living God whom we love, and we do so with joy because there's no greater joy than knowing him (Ps. 16:11).

Want to Know the Bible? Join a Church

Alright, let's get to the main question of this book: How can we get more out of our Bible reading? How can we read Scripture better? The first thing I'm going to suggest might surprise you. If you want to read the Bible better, join a local church.

"But wait," you think, "what does *that* have to do with reading the Bible? Shouldn't we start with a few tips for what I should be looking for in the Bible? How about a few practical suggestions? What about principles for interpretation?"

We'll get there a bit later. First, we need to consider something even more fundamental. God doesn't want his people holed-up in cubicles reading Scripture only for themselves. Instead, when God saves us, he makes us part of a people (Col. 1:13–14; 1 Pet. 2:10). He calls us to join a church—a community of fellow Bible readers. When we join a local church, we're committing to live according to God's word and in fellowship with his people. God saves us *into* his church and, in turn, the church points us back to God, the gospel, and Scripture. So if you want to learn the Bible, join a local church—God's school for Bible instruction.

Are you a little shocked by this claim? Let's think about it a little more. God's word should be at the heart of every church because God's word *creates* the church. God's word creates God's people who in turn hear and commit to following God's word. That sentence has a lot packed into it, so let's break it down.

We humans are spiritually dead in our sins (Eph. 2:1–3). We've sinned (Rom. 3:23), and we're therefore all subject to God's wrath (John 3:36; Rom. 6:23). But God in his grace sent his Son Jesus Christ, God in the flesh, to save us (John 1:1–14). Jesus lived a perfect life, died on our behalf, paid the penalty for our sins, and then rose from the dead as proof that his sacrifice for sin had been accepted (Rom. 3:21–26; 1 Pet. 2:21–25). Christians have proclaimed this good news of salvation through Christ alone for generations. All who call on his name, repent of their sins, and believe in him will be saved (Rom. 10:9–17; cf. John 6:35).

We learn all of this through God's word. It comes to us when we're dead in our sins. We hear it, and through the Spirit we're made alive. We turn from sin and turn to Christ in faith.

When this happens, God's people are not only reconciled to God; they're reconciled to one another. The animosity between humans that's raged since Cain killed Abel now ends. When we come to Christ, we link arms with others who've done the same. We come to Christ not only to obey everything he has commanded but also to help other Christians walk the same path of obedience. God's word gathers the church, and God's word instructs the church.

We were never meant to read the Bible in isolation. We're not supposed to try and figure it all out on our own. God doesn't expect all of us to be "Bible experts." But he does want all of us to read his word profitably and share it with others (Col. 3:16). We can do that as we learn to read Scripture with others in our local church.

Oddly, some people feel like they can be *too* dependent on the church for their spiritual growth—as if it's somehow "cheating" to be more encouraged by sermons than our personal devotions. Some people assume only young or particularly weak Christians need the local church. But nothing could be further from the truth. All Christians—young and old, immature and mature—need the oversight and instruction of a local church. We're not weak to rely on God's gifts in the church. God designed it to be this way. His word created the church, and now the church upholds and teaches his people his word.

Okay, let's get practical. How exactly does joining a local church help you read the Bible better?

The Church's Confession and Covenant

Luke stopped by my office for advice.[1] He had plans to move to a new community, and he was nervous. He had no clue what church to join. We hopped online to see what churches were in the area.[2] Like any good professor, I couldn't resist turning this moment into a little impromptu examination: "What's the first thing we should look at on these church websites?" Without hesitation (and to my great satisfaction) he responded, "The statement of faith."

Every church has a "statement of faith"— a confession that describes what they believe. Many churches also have a covenant that describes how they intend to live out their faith together as a community. In short, a statement of faith summarizes what a church thinks the Bible teaches about the things we should believe, and a church covenant summarizes what a church thinks the Bible teaches about how we should live.

How churches actually use these documents varies wildly. Some regularly read portions of their statement of faith on Sunday mornings. Some churches read their church covenant every time they take the Lord's Supper. At the very least, your church probably taught you the statement of faith when you first joined.

Regrettably, Christians often don't recognize the value of these documents, particularly when it comes to helping them read their Bibles. Think about it. The Bible's a big book. It's hard to keep all the big ideas straight. But a church confession and covenant summarizes most of the important teachings of the Bible in just a couple of pages. If we're regularly rehearsing our churches confession and covenant, we'll have the Bible's "big picture" in mind every time we open up the word.

Think of it this way: a church confession and covenant gives us guardrails for reading Scripture. These documents summarize Scripture's main teachings about God, the gospel, humanity, sin, Christ, salvation, the Holy Spirit, the church, and how we're supposed to live as people who await the return of Christ. They keep us from seeing things in Scripture that aren't there. Some might object: Why would we put such high priority on extra-biblical documents? But confessions and covenants emerge *from Scripture* in order to *point us back to Scripture*. They summarize the Bible so that we can be better readers of it; they don't replace it.

The Ministry of Preaching

Megan couldn't hide her enthusiasm for the Bible. She came up to me after church to tell me everything was finally starting to "click." After several years of sitting under sound preaching she began to notice how her pastor interpreted, explained, and applied the Bible. By simply showing up to church week after week, she had learned how to read Scripture by watching the example of her pastor.

The primary way local churches teach people to read their Bibles better is through preaching.

According to Scripture, pastors (also sometimes called "elders") are gifts from Christ to his church. Their primary job is to teach and preach the Bible. Just consider a bit of what the Bible says about pastors and elders.

- They must be "able to teach" (1 Tim. 3:2).
- They've been commissioned to proclaim the truth of God's word (2 Tim. 4:1–2).
- They're called to equip the saints so they can also engage in word-centered ministry (Eph. 4:11–16).

- They are men gifted by God both to teach Scripture and model obedience to it (Titus 2:7–8).

If the local church is God's school for Bible instruction, then pastors are gifted by God to teach in his school. If you want to become a better Bible reader, then avail yourself to God's good gift of pastors.

As you seek to learn Scripture better by sitting under a faithful preaching ministry, here are a few things to remember.

First, biblical preaching affirms that the Bible is the inspired, inerrant, and authoritative word of God (2 Tim. 3:16–17; 2 Pet. 1:20–21). If any pastor minimizes the importance of Scripture, even if unintentionally through what he does and doesn't emphasize, then find another church to join. You likely won't learn much about the Bible there.

Second, the most nourishing preaching is *expository preaching*, that is, preaching that *exposes* the meaning of the text and makes the point of the text the point of the sermon. In fact, expository preachers usually spend weeks or months (or maybe even years!) preaching verse-by-verse through whole books of the Bible. There's no better way to learn how to read Scripture than a weekly diet of expository preaching.

Third, as my friend Megan mentioned, faithful preaching won't just explain the content of Scripture but will also model how to read Scripture well. Good preachers take any unnecessary mystery out of interpreting the Bible. They show you how to read a passage in context and understand what it means. They also show you how it relates to the gospel and how to apply it to your life. Good preachers "show their homework" so that church members can read Scripture more capably. As you watch pastors interpret, explain, and apply the text Sunday after Sunday, you'll learn how to do the same.

If you truly want to become a better Bible reader, find a church that teaches the Bible and practices expository preaching.[3]

The Ministry of Teaching

While God gives pastors as the church's primary Bible teachers, other Christians also teach us the

Bible. Most churches provide additional opportunities for instruction: adult Bible classes, small groups, or men's and women's Bible studies.

These other teaching ministries often provide an opportunity for us to ask questions, provide our own biblical insights, and talk with fellow members about what we are learning. In the class I co-lead at my church, I frequently begin by asking folks to share something they read from the Bible that week, what it means, and how they're applying it to their lives. This practice has become a part of our church's culture, and people often come ready to share.

In such environments, members not only hear a lesson based on God's word, they also get to hear fellow church members share what they're learning about God in his word. Moments like these are simply one way we carry out the Bible's command to "instruct one another" (Rom. 15:14) as we learn from each other how to read Scripture better.

If you want to get more out of the Bible, avail yourself to your church's formal teaching ministries in addition to the Sunday sermon.

The Ministry of Fellowship and Discipleship

Sermons, formal classes, and small groups aren't the only ways the church teaches us to read Scripture better. We'll also become better Bible readers by simply investing in relationships with fellow members.

Christian fellowship centers around our shared commitment to Jesus and the gospel. We are united in Christ even if we are separated by gender, ethnicity, and socio-economic status. Despite all of our differences, Christ has formed us into a new humanity committed to living in biblical solidarity (Eph. 2:18–19) and speaking the truth in love (Eph. 4:15).

What does this mean practically? Well, when Christians hang out they tend to talk about the Bible. Of course, Christians have their share of opinions about sports, work, hobbies, and politics. But if you're around mature Christians, it won't be long until you hear someone start connecting the Bible to their daily life. Perhaps a sister shares about her parenting struggles and how a particular promise from Scripture is encouraging her. Maybe a brother mentions how what he's been reading in Matthew has helped his struggle with anxiety. At soccer fields, in the backyard, or over the dinner table, Christians share the faith they hold in common and often unintentionally teach one another the Bible (Rom. 15:14).

The benefit of these relationships for understanding Scripture has certainly proved true in my own life. For instance, some time ago I visited my friend Aaron's house for a Super Bowl party. We enjoyed some of the game, plenty of hilarious commercials, and an abundance of good food. But what I recall most about that night is our conversations about the Bible, theology, and how it all applied to our lives. None of it was planned—it's just something that happens when Christians get together. I left that party loving Jesus more than when I came in. I left that party knowing the Bible better than when I had first arrived. That simple act of Christian fellowship drove me back to God's word with greater understanding and affection.

But we don't just learn Scripture in infor
mal Christian fellowship. We also learn to rea
Scripture better through intentional disciplir
relationships. Discipling means helping othe
learn from Jesus so that they can follow Jesu
more faithfully.

If you're not in a discipling relationship, yo
should be! Jesus calls all of us to go and mak
disciples who follow him and to teach the
disciples to obey all that he commanded (Mat
28:19–20). Jesus wants us to be discipled an
disciple others. If you need help getting starte
in discipling relationships check out Garre
Kell's *How Can I Find Someone to Disciple M*
in this series.[4]

Are you struggling to understand the Bibl
Why not ask a mature Christian to meet fo
lunch once a week to read a book of the Bib
with you and to explain how he reads it?

Want to sharpen your reading skills so yo
can see more of what Scripture says? Get with
group of peers to read and discuss what you'
reading for your devotional time. Maybe even a
a pastor or elder in your church to meet with yo

Are you struggling in a particular area of life? Why not ask a mature believer to apply the Bible to your life and help you see how Scripture speaks to your situation?

But don't just look for those who can help you. Who can *you* help? Find someone in your church who needs discipling, reach out, and meet with him or her to talk through the Bible together. I regularly mentor several young men in this way. I hope they benefit from the time we have together. But they're not the only ones benefitting from our relationship. I'm amazed how these young men regularly increase my love for God and my knowledge of the word even as I strive to help them do the same.

Models of Obedience

Another way fellow church members help us read our Bibles better is by modeling obedience. Scripture's vision of the Christian life comes alive in God's people. In the local church, we witness people living out the commands of Scripture.

We get a front-row seat to watch others trust Christ's promises.

The Bible demands that we not be hearers of the word only, but doers (James 1:22). Observing others obey Scripture helps us understand and obey it. This isn't just a clever idea I came up with. Imitating the faith of others is all over the Bible. Scripture regularly calls us to observe how others obey God's commands and follow after them. We imitate them as they imitate Christ (1 Cor. 4:14–17; 11:1; Phil. 3:12–17; 4:8–9; 1 Thess. 1:4–7; 2 Thess. 3:6–9; Heb. 13:7).

Imitation comes quite naturally to us. When my children were young and needed to be spoon fed, my wife would humorously imitate them when they opened their mouth to take a bite. I would tease her but often found myself doing the exact same thing. As they grow older, children imitate their parents—whether through their accent, their hobbies, or even their wardrobe (my son still loves to coordinate with me). My wife and I often hear my daughter Hannah say things that we know she heard from us (this trait can be good or bad). My son loves to ride his bike with bike shorts and a jersey because he sees me doing it. No person remains uninfluenced. Imitation is inevitable, so we need to make sure we're imitating the right people.

The church provides us models of obedience that show us how to understand and apply Scripture. Here are just a few examples:

- Want to know what Paul means when he says "Love your wife like Christ loves the church" (see Eph. 5:25)? Look at a man in your church who models what it means to be a godly leader in his home.
- Want to know what it means when Jesus says cut off your hand if it causes you to stumble (Matt. 5:30)? Look at the guy in your small group who got rid of all his Internet devices in an effort to cut off any access to illicit material.
- Want to know what it means when Paul commands us to put away bitterness and empty rivalries (Phil. 2:1–4)? Look at those two elderly women sitting in the next pew who don't compare themselves to one another or take offense

at one another's foolish comments from the past, but continue to serve each other despite their differences.

As God's school for Bible instruction, the church teaches us how to rightly interpret the Scriptures and also models—albeit imperfectly—how to live it out.

Reading Scripture for the Sake of Others

Here's one final consideration for how the church teaches you to read Scripture: your Bible reading is not just about you!

What you read each day in private and what you hear in services each week at your local church is meant to reverberate through you into your church community. The preacher stewards and heralds the word so that we become stewards and heralds of that same word. We may never do that through formal teaching, but every church member has numerous opportunities to read the Bible with others in mind and then speak biblical truth to them: "Speak the truth

[to] his neighbor, for we are members one of another" (Eph. 4:25; see also Eph. 4:15–16, 29).

I need to speak the Bible to others, and I need to have it spoken to me.

It may surprise you, but the world of competitive cycling illustrates this point. I love cycling. The bike trails near my house go in various directions for hundreds of miles. For a long time, I mostly rode alone. But after a couple of years, I decided to enter an event that would involve about a thousand riders.

At the starting line, I saw a friend who knew I was new to competitive cycling. He leaned over and told me, "Take advantage of the drafting. Get a couple feet behind the bike in front of you—it reduces air resistance by like 30 percent." As I settled into the event, I joined a group of about ten riders. I couldn't believe how much easier it was to go the distance simply by drafting others around me!

When people speak the word of God into my life, it has a similar drafting effect. It helps me as I run the race of the Christian life.

Paul tells us to let the word of Christ dwell in us richly as we teach and admonish one another with all wisdom (Col. 3:16). You see, God wants all of us to be word-filled people who regularly encourage and instruct one another from the Bible. This requires reading and hearing that goes beyond our own individual lives.

When we learn to read Scripture in the church, we remember that we're reading Scripture not to bolster our knowledge and puff ourselves up through our own great insights. Rather, we read Scripture to serve one another with the word— our family, our friends, our small group. We read Scripture for the good of others as much as we read for the good of ourselves.

A Few Tips for Better Bible Reading

The most important thing you can do to learn to read your Bible better is join a church. Now that we've established this foundation, I want to offer a few practical suggestions you can start using *right now* as you read your Bible. Again, you'll find all of this modeled in the church, but let me give you a few ideas of what you should be on the lookout for.

We need to keep three questions before us at all times as we read the Bible.

- What is the Bible all about?
- What is the book all about?
- What is this passage all about?

These questions will come into play as we consider the following four principles for better Bible reading.

Principle 1: Understand the Bible's Big Picture

First, before you get into the all details, think about the overall storyline of the Bible. In other words, what's the whole Bible all about?

When The Lord of the Rings movies came out in the early 2000s, I recall being at a showing of *The Two Towers*, the second of the three films. I saw a friend at the theater, and we shared our mutual excitement. He then confessed something rather strange: He'd neither read the books nor seen the first film. I was confused. Why hadn't he watched the first one before coming to see the second? Sure enough, when I saw him afterward, he was thoroughly perplexed. He didn't know the big picture, so he couldn't understand what was happening. The same lesson applies to reading the Bible well. We need the big picture.

So what *is* the Bible's big story? This may surprise you, but you can actually summarize the whole Bible in six words:

- **Creation**: God made all things out of nothing (Gen. 1:1–2:3).
- **Fall**: Humanity rebeled against God; sin and death entered the world (Gen. 3:1–24).
- **Israel:** As God's chosen people in the Old Testament, Israel was called to keep the covenant and live holy lives. Ultimately, they failed and were exiled from their land (Genesis 12–Malachi 4).
- **Salvation:** Jesus came. As God in the flesh, he lived a perfect life, died in our place, bore God's wrath against our sin, and rose again, offering us salvation from our sin by faith alone in him (Matthew—John).
- **Church:** The people of God who were saved by faith in Christ gather into local assemblies to commemorate the gospel and oversee one

another's membership through biblical preaching and the ordinances (Acts—Jude).

- **New Creation:** Christ will return and consummate his kingdom. Sin, Satan, and death will be done away with forever. There will be no more crying, pain, or sorrow, and we will be with God as his people joyfully worshiping him forever (Revelation).

That's the storyline of the Bible in a nutshell.

That story plays out across various *covenants* in which God makes "big promises" to his people. Think of each covenant as the "next episode" in redemption's unfolding saga. God's covenant with Adam established God's relationship with humanity. Adam, as God's image bearer, must obey God and represent his righteous rule. But Adam rebelled against God, so all humanity suffers the consequences of death and sin (Genesis 1–3). In his covenant with Noah, God promised not to destroy humanity as he did in the flood and assured humanity that he would preserve creation while he worked out the history of redemption (Genesis 8–9).

In the Abrahamic covenant God chose Abraham and his children as his covenant people. He promised them land, offspring, and blessing. He also promised to bless the nations through Abraham's family (Genesis 12; 15; 17). In the Mosaic covenant, God redeemed Israel from slavery in Egypt and gave them his law, requiring that they be a kingdom of priests and a holy nation before the Lord (Exodus 19–24). In the Davidic Covenant, God promised David that a king would come from his line whose kingdom would last forever and who would bring about the blessing to the nations promised to Abraham (2 Samuel 7).

Finally, God promised a new covenant, which would fulfill all the others. In this new covenant, the Messiah, the king from David's line, would fulfill all of God's promises and create a new people of God. These people are indwelt by the Holy Spirit, their sins are forgiven, and they have the law of God written on their hearts (Jer. 31:31–34). These covenants are the backbone of the biblical storyline, taking us from creation to new creation. If we're going to interpret the Bible rightly, we always need to remember *where* we are in the story and how each covenant unfolds God's redemptive plan.

Ultimately, this little survey emphasizes one important point: The Bible is a story. Certainly, it contains commands, promises, wisdom, and several other genres. But at its heart, Scripture is a story that's ultimately fulfilled in Jesus. We could summarize that story in one sentence: God is establishing his kingdom through covenants, climaxing in Christ, all for his glory.

If you want to read Scripture well, you always need to remember the big picture and know exactly where you are in the storyline.

Principle 2: See What's There

Have you ever heard the story of "Agassiz and the Fish." It's a story of a college student wanting to study with Agassiz, a renowned zoology professor. When the student lets Agassiz know of his desire, the professor pulls a jar with a fish inside off the shelf and tells the student to look at it.

At various points, Agassiz quizzes the student. He asks him to offer his observations on the fish. At first, the professor is disappointed with the student's responses, chastising him for seeing so little. The student continues to observe, staring at the fish for hours. He takes notes. He draws the fish. He does everything he can to see what's there. Eventually, Agassiz commends him for his observations. But the exhortation was always the same, no matter what animal lay before the student: "Look, look, look."[5]

We all need a day with Agassiz to learn how to study our Bibles. There's no special shortcut for understanding Scripture. We simply have to keep looking at the text, and looking at the text, and looking at the text. We have to see what's there—and that task takes time.

So what are some ways we can see what's actually there in the text?

First, Read the Bible Fast

Reading a whole book of the Bible in one sitting helps you grasp its overall message. That's easy to do for a book like Jude or Philippians. It's a much bigger challenge if you want to tackle Deuteronomy or Isaiah. But it's well worth your time—a worthy substitute for a Netflix binge! If you read a book of the Bible in segments over a period of days, you'll miss a ton of connections. But if you read it in one sitting, you'll start to see what an author is doing with the overall book.

Along with reading a whole book in one sitting, you should also read it through multiple times. We'll never see all there is to see in one go. So if you want to improve your Bible reading, pick a book and read it several times. As you do, write a one-sentence summary for each chapter. Then when you're done, write a one-sentence summary of the whole book. This will get you on your way to understanding what the book is about.

Second, Read the Bible Slowly

In order to get a sense of a whole book, read it fast. But if you want to start getting into the weeds of a particular book, then you need to read slowly . . . really slowly. You'll need to find a way to focus on a chapter or even a paragraph. One practice you might consider is taking a paragraph of the Bible and writing it out by hand. Practices like this help us slow down and *see what's there*.

"Okay," you say, "I'm reading slowly and really trying to see what's there. What should I be looking for?" Here are some helpful tips to consider.

- Remember: Context is king! Try to figure out how the paragraph you're studying contributes to the argument of the book. Always remember to locate where you are in the biblical storyline. What covenants have come before? How does that shape your understanding of the passage? What covenants and promises come after what you're reading, and how should that shape your understanding?
- Look for repeated words.
- Look for clear commands.
- If you're reading a narrative—like a story from the Old Testament or something from the Gospels or Acts—look for places where either the narrator or one of the main characters inserts his own commentary into the story. For example, if Jesus tells us the meaning of one of his parables, we don't need to go looking for another meaning; he already interpreted it for us!

- Look for key words (e.g., *therefore, for, so that, however,* etc.), and think about how they connect sentences and ideas.
- Look to see how other authors of Scripture understand the passage you're studying. For instance, if you're trying to understand Joel 2, read Peter's interpretation of it in Acts 2. The more you read the New Testament, you'll find that the New Testament authors are regularly quoting and explaining the Old Testament and showing how it's fulfilled in Jesus.
- Always remember, let the clear parts of the Bible interpret the unclear parts.
- Try to memorize Scripture. You'll be shocked by how much you notice in a passage you've committed to memory.

Remember, the point is to *see what's there* and to *just keep looking*.

Third, Ask Good Questions

Another way to see what's in the text is to ask questions. We want to bombard each passage of Scripture with questions. Here's a list of the types of questions you should bring to every passage of Scripture:

- Who are the main characters? What are they doing?
- What are the main themes of this passage?
- Does this passage teach anything about an important doctrine?
- What does this text reveal about God?
- What does this text say about sin?
- What does this text say about the world?
- Does this passage contain any commands?
- Does this passage contain any promises?

You can ask any number of questions of the passage your reading. The point isn't to ask a specific set of questions. The point is that you should be an inquisitive reader. Keep looking at the text, keep asking questions. See what's there.

Principle 3: Understand the Meaning

These tips on observation are aimed at two things: interpreting and applying the Bible. Ultimately, we want to observe what's *there* so we can understand the original author's intention. What did he mean when he wrote these words? All of our observations should aim at answering that question. As you seek to uncover that meaning, here are a few more principles to help you along the way:

- Know that there are different types of writing in the Bible (e.g., narrative, poetry, prophecy, letters) and seek to understand them accordingly. Realize that the way you interpret a book of poetry is different than how you interpret a book of history.
- Always consider context. Read each verse in light of the chapter, read each chapter in light of the whole book, and ultimately read each book in light of the whole Bible.
- Look up key words to determine their specific meanings.
- Identify any figurative language in your passage, and seek to understand it within its context.
- Correlate your findings with related passages in Scripture.

- Use other tools, such as commentaries, theology books, and your church's confession to serve as guardrails for your interpretation.

Every biblical author has a specific intention. We don't want to read our own meaning into the text. We want to draw out from the text what the author meant to say to his readers.

Principle 4: Apply Truth to Life

Once we've observed what's in the text and uncovered its meaning, we want to apply the truth of Scripture to our lives. We can do that by asking four questions:

- What does God want me to believe?
- What does God want me to love?
- What does God want me to desire?
- What does God want me to do?

The Bible is meant to shape our minds (Rom. 12:1–2; Phil. 4:8), our affections (Eph. 5:1–2), our yearnings (Ps. 73:25–26), and our actions (1 Pet. 1:13–16). As we behold the glory of the

Lord in his word (2 Cor. 3:18–4:4), we're increasingly and incrementally transformed into his image. As we repent of sin and turn to the gospel, God really does produce spiritual fruit in our lives.

A Community of Bible Readers

I pastored in Wisconsin for several years. I met a man named Paul there; he became one of my closest friends. Paul was by all accounts "a regular guy." He was married, worked 9-to-5, and enjoyed a few hobbies like hunting and fishing. When I first met him, he'd been to church occasionally but wasn't particularly grounded in his understanding of the Christian faith. But as he committed to our church, something started to change. He began to listen carefully to the sermons, attend Bible studies, and read Scripture on a daily basis. As our families spent more time together, he would share what he was reading in Scripture and how it was changing him. He began to read theology books and started to teach Bible studies. Eventually, he became a lay-elder in the church—a post he's held ever since.

On numerous occasions, Paul told me that becoming a meaningful member of our church changed his life and his understanding of Scripture forever. He was always quick to mention that it wasn't because of someone's personality or some special program in the church. Rather, it was the community—a community built around the word of God. Scripture reverberated from the pulpit through the teaching ministries and discipling relationships into our ordinary, day-to-day lives. It echoed through us to those in the community who needed to hear the gospel. It rang throughout our relationships Monday through Saturday as the church scattered to its various places and stations. And it would crescendo as we would gather once again as God's people on Sunday morning.

Friend, I want you to get more out of your Bible. I want you to make Scripture an immovable priority in your life. So join a local church that's committed to upholding and adoring God's word.

Joyfully meditate on Scripture day and night (Ps. 1:1–3) in the context of your local church so that you can continually behold the glory of God and so be transformed into his image (2 Cor. 3:18).

Recommended Resources

For further reading on how the local church teaches us to read Scripture well, check out:

Mark Dever. *Discipling: How to Help Others Follow Jesus*. Wheaton, IL: Crossway, 2016.

Jonathan Leeman. *Word-Centered Church: How Scripture Brings Life and Growth to God's People*. Wheaton, IL: Crossway, 2017.

For further reading on how to interpret and apply Scripture, check out:

J. Scott Duvall and J. Daniel Hays. *Grasping God's Word: A Hands-On Approach to Reading, Interpreting, and Applying the Bible*. 3rd Edition. Grand Rapids, MI: Zondervan, 2012.

Graeme Goldsworthy. *According to Plan: The Unfolding Revelation of God in the Bible*. Downers Grove, IL: InterVarsity Press, 1991.

Robert Plummer. *40 Questions on Interpreting the Bible*. Grand Rapids, MI: Kregel, 2010.

Vaughn Roberts. *God's Big Picture: Tracing the Storyline of the Bible*. Downers Grove, IL: InterVarsity Press, 2002.

Notes

1. Personal stories involving other individuals are shared in this booklet with permission from those individuals. Often pseudonyms have been used for privacy.
2. For helpful lists of churches that ascribe to the teachings found in this series of booklets, check out https://www.9marks.org/church-search/ and https://www.thegospelcoalition.org/churches/.
3. If you want to learn more about expository preaching, check out David Helm, *Expositional Preaching: How We Speak God's Word Today* (Wheaton, IL: Crossway, 2014).
4. Garrett Kell, *How Can I Find Someone to Disciple Me?* Church Questions (Wheaton, IL: Crossway, 2021).
5. For the full, fascinating story, see Justin Taylor, "Agassiz and the Fish," TGC blog, November 16, 2009, https://www.thegospelcoalition.org/blogs/justin-taylor/agassiz-and-the-fish/, which quotes the original source: Samuel H. Scudder, "Agassiz and the Fish, by a Student" *American Poems*, 3rd ed. (Boston: Houghton, Osgood & Co., 1879), 450–54.

Scripture Index

Scripture Index

IX 9Marks

Building Healthy Churches

9Marks exists to equip church leaders with a biblical vision and practical resources for displaying God's glory to the nations through healthy churches.

To that end, we want to see churches characterized by these nine marks of health:

1. Expositional Preaching
2. Gospel Doctrine
3. A Biblical Understanding of Conversion and Evangelism
4. Biblical Church Membership
5. Biblical Church Discipline
6. A Biblical Concern for Discipleship and Growth
7. Biblical Church Leadership
8. A Biblical Understanding of the Practice of Prayer
9. A Biblical Understanding and Practice of Missions

Find all our Crossway titles and other resources at 9Marks.org.

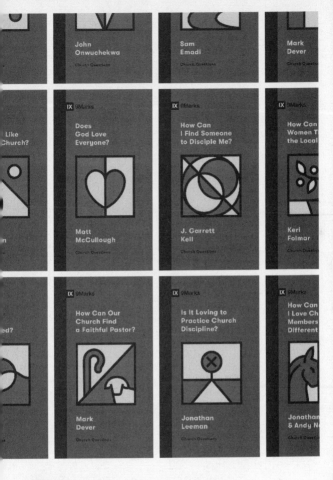

John Onwuchekwa
Church Questions

Sam Emadi
Church Questions

Mark Dever
Church Questions

Like Church?

Does God Love Everyone?

How Can I Find Someone to Disciple Me?

How Can Women T the Local

Matt McCullough
Church Questions

J. Garrett Kell
Church Questions

Keri Folmar
Church Questions

How Can Our Church Find a Faithful Pastor?

Is It Loving to Practice Church Discipline?

How Can I Love Ch Members Different

Mark Dever
Church Questions

Jonathan Leeman
Church Questions

Jonathan & Andy N
Church Questions

IX 9Marks Church Questions

Providing ordinary Christians with sound and accessible biblical teaching by answering common questions about church life.

For more information, visit crossway.org.